The 13 Most Dangerous Traffic Situations

and

How to Survive Them

Mitch Terrusa

Copyright © 2014 Mitch Terrusa

Terrusa Publishing (TerrusaPublishing.com)

ISBN-10: 1497596580
ISBN-13: 978-1497596580

DEDICATION

Sal Terrusa created a top driving school in California named Teen Auto Club spanning 21 years.

Teen Auto Club was a driving school with high quality standards and dedicated to traffic safety, instilling excellence in driving in it's students.

Mr. Terrusa's program is presented here so that generations to come can benefit from the life-saving skills he promoted.

CONTENTS

ACKNOWLEDGMENTS

Sal Terrusa gathered together a fine team to carry out his dream that made Teen Auto Club such a successful program. His wife Jo was instrumental in devising systems and gave her support throughout Teen Auto Club's existence.

Excellent instructors committed to making and keeping our reputation for the highest standards such as John Stapley, Kathleen Smith, Tom Young, Myk Price, Carl Lionarons and Narcy "Mario" Duliere helped turn the dream into reality.

John Stapley is still teaching driver training and his experience, professionalism and dedication to driver safety could have no better champion. Carry on, John.

Dozens of instructors who came through our school were instrumental in carrying the mission and entrusted to teach our students. Our talented and caring office staff did their part to keep customer service to our students as their primary focus.

THE 13 MOST DANGEROUS TRAFFIC SITUATIONS

AND HOW TO SURVIVE THEM

PRELUDE

In my early life, I was a Master Instructor and along with teaching driver education and training, I was tasked with the job of teaching driving instructors how to teach students how to drive. It may have been low-pay, high-risk work but as long as we valued the mission behind the work – to help people survive driving – it was a very worthwhile career.

The core of our driver training program was based on The 13 Most Dangerous Traffic Situations and before you get bored and bleary-eyed, let me ask you this:

If I were able to help you learn how to eliminate 95% of all the bad things that could happen to you on the road, would you be interested?

If you are, I will give you simple, easy-to-follow methods to help you make your driving skills even better than they already are.

If you are under 44 years old, driving is the biggest threat to your life, statistically. If you're over 44 it will always remain a big threat.

First, you must realize that 95% of all drivers *think* they are better drivers than average. Don't believe me? Ask 10 people. Ask 100.

While it is mathematically impossible for 95% of all drivers to be better than average, I can guarantee that, if you follow the methods for eliminating the 13 most dangerous traffic situations, you can honestly claim to be better than average. In fact, if you make all these skills part of your regular driving pattern, you will be in the top 5%.

THE NATURE OF HABITS

We live most of our lives automatically stepping through a series of pre-programmed – pre-learned patterns of behavior – called habits.

Habits usually fall into two categories:

1. **Good Habits: Those habits that tend uplift, enhance, or protect us.**

2. **Bad Habits: Those habits that tend to diminish, destroy, or put us at risk.**

Our eating habits tend to keep us healthy or unhealthy. We make nearly unconscious choices every day and we have a habit of choosing the things we've chosen before.

We may think that we make conscious choices each day but that is not completely true because we decide to do or try something originally and then we make a habit of it and no longer really think about the choices we make. We just select out of habit. These patterns of behavior are how we are wired. We tend to do things over and over because we have tried them before and it didn't cause us discomfort. In fact, it probably gave us some level of pleasure which is why we repeat the behavior and turn it into a habit.

There are good habits and bad habits determined by their short or long term effect on our health and survival. We usually get immediate pleasure from bad habits and that is why so many of us develop them. They are bad because they don't support good health or are risky in some way. We can usually get away with some bad behavior if it is occasional but chronic abuse of anything will increase the risk and will usually take its toll in time.

Habits in driving follow the same rules:

a) Good habits will tend to protect us.

b) Bad habits will tend to put us at risk.

When we first learn to drive we are creating habits and the quality of the habits will determine our survival rate. If we have learned to drive, picking up some bad habits along the way, we have put ourselves, our passengers and other drivers at risk.

Once a bad habit is developed it takes a tremendous amount of self-discipline to replace the habit with a good one. When I was teaching new instructors I learned just how hard it is to take good drivers and make them great drivers and then have them develop the skills to teach these habits to new drivers. It is so much easier to teach new drivers because they have not learned bad habits. Experienced drivers have to replace bad habits with good habits and it is amazing how resistant to change we are as drivers.

A wonderful thing about habits is that they take very little effort to maintain. We do them automatically. We don't have to think about it. So if our habits are good, we don't have to make any effort to follow them. <u>The key is to create the good habit in the first place</u>. Once in place, we don't have to remember it because we always do it the same way. Good habits will tend to protect us even if we are not paying conscious attention to them.

It is the nature of driving (as it is with all habits) that we do them automatically. The skills I will present to you will have to be done consciously for a time until they become an automatic part of your driving and then seep into your automatic skills. You might need to revisit these a few times to be sure you are still using them so keep them handy.

If I am catching you at a time in your life when you are just beginning to drive, these skills will be easy to master because you will be learning good skills from the beginning. If you have been driving for a time it will take the overcoming of basic ego and a commitment to be open to a better and safer way of driving. That is no small matter so I congratulate you in advance for your efforts. You may have to unlearn some skills and replace them with skills designed to keep you and your precious passengers alive.

I hope to help you live life to the fullest by not having it cut short simply because you didn't know simple but important driving techniques to keep you alive. You might know some of these, but I have never met anyone who knew them all without this training. It doesn't hurt anything if you already know these skills and it confirms what a good driver you already are.

Realize that you don't control anyone but yourself. Even if you are the best driver in the world, that makes everyone else less capable than you and you have to defend yourself from the mistakes, the carelessness and the lack of skill by other drivers. So driving defensively is a life-saving skill. Every driver makes mistakes. You must compensate for the mistakes of others because it doesn't matter if you're "in-the-right" if you get killed – except to your estate. Learning these skills and making them habits will give you a much better chance of survival.

Most accidents are avoidable. I know this statement makes people – particularly those who have been in an accident, a bit defensive, but the reality is that most accidents -- 95% of them -- could be avoided if just one of the drivers involved had been using these defensive driving techniques.

The purpose of driving is to get from one place to another in a safe, efficient and economical manner. Safe driving is a cooperative activity since we share the road with others. There is no place on our roads and highways where driving should be a competition. That is the first sign that a driver is a poor driver. Getting the mind on the right track takes maturity and sense. Age doesn't determine that. I have taught 15 and 16 year olds with the maturity and sense needed to be an excellent driver. I have witnessed much older drivers who are far too immature to be responsible drivers.

Competitive driving should be done when the driver is properly trained, in vehicles designed for competition with safety cages and protective racing gear. Then, it should be restricted to race tracks and roads set aside for such activity with other trained professional drivers.

MY BEST FRIEND

I came to driving instruction as a profession being motivated to do so after my best friend, Marilyn, was injured in a car accident. She had been driving for many years and never had a traffic ticket or accident before this one. She was a good driver.

She was a top teacher, dearly loved by her students and dedicated to making sure they were well prepared to enter their adult lives. The years of dedication she gave to her students did not go unappreciated. They knew she cared about them, loved them and wanted the best for them. They returned her affection by throwing parties for her and writing her thank-you's. Some honored her by returning in later years to thank her for the positive influence she had been to them as her teacher, mentor and friend.

Marilyn loved life and her fun and exuberant life-force carried her through long days and long nights of two jobs and grading papers. She raised two sons, often with the help of her mother and father when they came out to California from Michigan and stayed a few months each year.

One winter morning on her way to San Pedro High School, she pulled out in the middle of an intersection and waited for traffic to clear as she did every weekday. The light changed to yellow and the traffic cleared. She started to go but her car needed a tune-up and it hesitated for a second.

At that moment, a 19 year-old man came speeding around the corner and saw the yellow light and hit the gas because he didn't want to be late for work. She saw him and hit the gas to get out of his way but it was too late.

His 57 Chevy struck the right rear quarter panel of her car at approximately 55 miles per hour and the light-body 1970 Torino GT convertible she was driving spun around 3 ½ times before coming to a stop against the curb. If he had not been speeding or if her car had been properly tuned, the accident could have been avoided.

Marilyn's hand flew off the steering wheel by the force of the collision and struck the rear-view mirror breaking it off with her knuckles. She was shaken but seemed okay and so did the 19 year-old speeder. Both cars were total losses.

She was sore from the accident but about 5 weeks later, she couldn't get out of bed. The pain of whiplash is real. Whiplash has a bad reputation because so many people fake having whiplash since it is soft tissue damage that can't be proven or disproven by x-rays. For those people that really have whiplash, it can be very painful. Six months after the accident, x-rays discovered that she had disintegrating discs in her spine from the accident – bone spurs had formed causing her a great deal of pain.

The pain was so debilitating that, even though the procedure of a laminectomy at the time of her surgery was considered very dangerous, she elected to have it.

Unfortunately, the surgery made the pain worse.

She tried everything available to stop the pain. From acupuncture to pain medications to chiropractic treatment, nothing could dull the pain enough for her to live a normal life.

After years of fighting the State of California for early retirement due to her disability; after having to give up her career, her home and most of her dreams, she won a small early retirement. It was not enough money to live on her own. Marilyn couldn't work anymore. She tried but she could not sustain working at any job through her pain. She was forced to move in with her mother in order to survive financially.

Over the years she tried to maintain a positive view but it was depressing for her to live with chronic pain and often, it got to her.

She couldn't stand, sit or lie down for more than 30 minutes at a time. The pain invaded her sleep. Once I found her asleep in a chair with a book in her hand. I adjusted her blanket and tried to remove the book from her hand. She had it in a very tense grip and I had to pry her fingers off the book to remove it.

I remember visiting her at her mother's house and found her drinking alcohol heavily while taking larger than prescribed doses of pain medications. I was alarmed. I told her that that combination might kill her. She looked me straight in the eye and with level seriousness and an angry catch in her voice revealing her frustration said, "Good."

She looked down with tears forming, ashamed of the honest but negative answer she gave me. She recovered herself and attempted to explain, "The constant pain is so great and I never have any time that I am free of it. I'm so frustrated by it and so exhausted by it that there are times when death looks like the only way I'll ever be free from hurting. I'm sorry that I'm not stronger than I am."

I flashed back to the 19-year old who didn't want to be late for work. How many of us make that choice to hit the gas when we shouldn't because we don't want to be late -- as if those 90 seconds we lose at the light matters more than life itself. That 90 seconds cost Marilyn a lifetime of pain.

That one decision -- to hit the gas on a yellow light -- caused the loss of a great teacher to all the future students she would never be able to teach. The decision to hit the gas caused Marilyn and her family financial ruin. The joy she used to bring to her family and friends never returned. Trying to save 90 seconds ended the vital dreams she had – dreams that would never be fulfilled.

90 Seconds.

She was 40 when she had the accident. She was in her prime. Marilyn's contribution to the world was stunted by a careless driver and an overdue tune-up.

In my view, the accident took her life; it just took her 17 years of frustrating agony to die.

Certainly, life as she knew it was over from that accident. Officially, it was cancer that took her life. I believe that her pain lowered her resistance to disease and her body couldn't fight the pain and cancer, too. She was 57.

You're free now, Marilyn.

When the opportunity came to join my father's fledgling driving school called **Teen Auto Club Driving School**, I thought about my best friend. I thought that I might be able to make a difference. If I could stop a young driver from making the same mistakes, then that would be a worthwhile use of my time and my life.

I decided to join him for that reason.

Marilyn was my best friend. She was an inspiration to her students. At the end of her life, she faced death courageously expressing the hope that death was just the next great adventure for her. She taught me how to live and, by her courage, how to die.

Marilyn was my best friend. She was also my mom.

TEEN AUTO CLUB DRIVING SCHOOL

I joined **Teen Auto Club** when we had one car and a wonderful high school girl named Theresa as a part-time bookkeeper. The success we had the first summer I joined was phenomenal. My father asked me to stay on into the Fall rather than return to school because there was more business than he could handle. I thought the work would taper off by Winter and I could return to school in the Spring. It didn't so I didn't return to school until much later.

The 13 Defensive Driving Techniques were created by Sal Terrusa over a period of time as a result of real-life events both as a driver and a high school driver education and training instructor. Other defensive driving programs have many of the same items but the ones that are most important and presented here have been selected for their effectiveness to real driving environment safety success.

These remained the core concepts that drove **Teen Auto Club** to the pinnacle of success it enjoyed from 1971 to 1992. One of the most highly regarded schools in the industry, **Teen Auto Club Driving School** enjoyed a stellar reputation for excellence in training, integrity of its system and the effectiveness of its program.

The ultimate mission of **Teen Auto Club** was to provide students with life-saving driving skills that would protect them for a lifetime of driving.

The thought that Teen Auto Club's core program was gone forever and of no life-saving benefit to anyone anymore after the closing of the driving school prompted me to write this guide so that people interested in safety while driving could benefit from the research and success of Teen Auto Club's program.

My Mission:

Until our vehicles drive themselves

and human skills are no longer required to safely drive,

I offer these life-saving skills behind one of the

most successful driver training programs ever.

THE 13 MOST DANGEROUS TRAFFIC SITUATIONS AND HOW TO SURVIVE THEM

SKILL # 1 INTERSECTION CONTROL

Cover your brake and look left and right through intersections.

It is a simple-to-master skill, but almost no one does it. Only the best drivers do. The momentum you have when you go through an intersection can carry you through while you cover the brake. You will lose no more than a 1 or 2 miles per hour on level ground in the 1 second you cover your brake. If you are in a residential area you will need to slow to as low as 15 mph at blind or uncontrolled intersections so you will probably have to break as you approach them.

Why cover your brake? You cover your brake to eliminate reaction time. The time it takes for you to see a problem, take you foot off the gas and step on your brake is called reaction time. The average reaction time is ¾ of a second. At 30 miles and hour you are traveling at 44 feet per second and in ¾ of a second you go 33 feet. Most accidents could be avoided by just a few feet and by covering your brake you effectively eliminate the time it takes to get to your brake. By reducing your stopping distance by 33 feet you could greatly reduce the accident's impact, damage and injury or avoid the collision altogether.

Let's break it down further. We look left first, because that is the lane of traffic that will hit you first if someone is running the light or stop sign. They would be wrong to do it but they could do it for any number of reasons: They could be drunk or stoned, or in a hurry, or they could be sick or unconscious or running from the police. The list of possible reasons is endless. You may have the right-of-way to go through the intersection but being right is not an effective bumper – being right doesn't prevent an accident. Defensive Driving skills do that.

Of all the skills I teach you, this one may be the hardest to learn. It will feel awkward and may even feel foolish, particularly since you've probably never seen anyone do it. This may be the first skill taught and because of it being awkward, the last skill learned, but if you do it until it becomes second nature and feels natural you will move head and shoulders above the drivers who refuse to master this technique. Without it you can't ever be more than a 90% better driver.

Note: Some may tell you that you should look 'Left - Right - Left' but that is true for pedestrians -- even bicyclists, and certainly when you are starting up after a stop sign. Left -Right - Left is not to be done by drivers who are traveling at better than 25 miles per hour most of the time -- there isn't time to look left again at higher speeds.

SKILL # 2 S-T-P: THE STATIONARY CHECK

Situation: You are first in line, waiting at a red light and the light turns to green. STP stands for:

1. **Signal**

2. **Traffic**

3. **Pedestrians**

There are three hazards to check for as you start up slowly (3 to 5 miles per hour). Be sure it is your signal that is green and not a left arrow only. Then check left and right to be sure traffic is stopping. Scan for pedestrians that may still be in the crosswalk because of infirmity of body or brain. They still have the right of way.

SKILL # 3 STOPPING POSITION

The third intersection defensive driving technique is to stop far enough behind the car in front of you to see the bottom of both tires. If you are first in line, stop far enough back to see the first limit line. By making this a part of your safe driving habits, you will occasionally have an advantage and increase your protection in case of a rear-end collision.

First, the advantage: If you observe people who come up to a red light behind another car, you will quickly see ordinary drivers who stop just a couple of feet behind the car in front. If that car or one in front stalled or otherwise became disabled, they would have to back up in order to change lanes to go around the vehicle. This is how entire lines of traffic can get stuck for a long time because everyone has pulled too closely and will have to back up. Only the last car in the line can back up, and does unless yet another ordinary driver pulls up too closely and figures things out too late.

As you become an extraordinary driver, however, having developed the habit of stopping far enough back of the car in front of you to see the bottom of the back tires, you can go around the vehicle in front without backing up because you have enough room to get around the vehicle, freeing yourself and all the drivers behind you at the same time instantly becoming a hero and also one who is on time!

The rear-end collision protection is also important and only has to save your life once to be worth doing. You have stopped far enough behind to see the bottom of both tires. Being an aware driver, you watch the person behind you approach in your rearview mirror. If that person is slumped over the steering wheel or waving his or her hands wildly in a "look out for me" fashion or leaping out of the car on the driver's side, you have an opportunity to pull off to the left or right and let them hit the poor ordinary driver in front of you. If you can't escape, you can at least prepare for a collision putting your head back against the head rest to limit whiplash and rest you foot lightly on the brake so you bounce forward, reducing the impact.

Since you have space in front of you, you might even avoid hitting the car in front altogether or at least reduce the damage to all vehicles by having that cushion.

SKILL # 4 THE POINT OF NO RETURN

The most dangerous place on the road is in the intersection. Nearly half of all accidents happen at intersections and over half of *those* involve a left turn. The most common accident involves a left hand turn at an intersection.

When is the most dangerous *time* at an intersection? When the light is changing, of course. Why? Because people waiting to make a left hand turn are trying to clear the intersection because they will soon be in the path of the cars with the new green light. This is a time when there is a real "On-your-mark, get-set, GO!" attitude for the left-turn drivers. The comic Gallagher used to joke that "If I am waiting to turn left, when the light turns yellow, it's MINE: I paid for it with my green!"

At the same time there is the same "Can I make it through the light before I get stuck at the red" attitude going on in the minds of the drivers who are approaching a 'stale' green light. A stale green light is a green light that has been green long enough to change to yellow at any moment.

So what do people do? That's right -- they hit the gas to make the green or yellow light.

They speed up in the most dangerous place at the most dangerous time with a foot on the gas!

Guilty? Yeah, well most of us are, occasionally. The average driver makes one ticketable mistake a mile. The odds of a bad habit catching up to you increase with the frequency of its exercise. Some people always do it. THIS is an accident waiting to happen.

You see it often – people hit the gas because they don't know if they have enough time to get through the light. Some drivers are indecisive and slam on their brakes when they discover they will not make it – sometimes skidding into the intersection. It's a wild world out there!

You do not control anyone but yourself, so how do you keep yourself protected going through an intersection?

First some things you need to know to understand:

-At 30 miles per hour you are traveling at 44 feet per second.

-A normal yellow light will stay yellow for at least 3 seconds

-In that time you will travel 132 feet.

Understanding that, if you pick a point that is about 100 feet (that's one normal light pole or two houses each on 50 foot lots) from the intersection and make that the "Point of No Return" you accomplish several things:

1. You eliminate indecision. At that point you commit to going through the intersection safely.

2. You can do so safely without hitting the gas because you know that you can cover the brake and look left and right and coast through the intersection and be well into the intersection (132' – 100' = 32') and have plenty of time to go through safely by the time the light turn red.

3. Safety is increased and stress is reduced.

Described precisely, *The Point of No Return* is the point you must reach before the light turns yellow or you will stop – but once reached you have plenty of time to go through the intersection safely covering you brake and looking left and right.

It's a peaceful thing once mastered. The Point of No Return is 100 feet from the intersection limit line at 30 miles per hour. If you are going faster, your Point of No Return has to be further from the intersection. At 40 miles per hour the Point of No Return is 132 feet. Roughly 30 feet more per 10 miles per hour increase.

I like to make a game of it. At 30 miles per hour, unless I get there –100 feet from the intersection - by the time the light turns yellow I'm going to stop.

Sometimes I reverse it – If I get there before the light turns yellow I'm going through. Either way works fine – just don't speed up to get to the Point of No Return.

SKILL # 5 HAZARDS ON THE RIGHT

Your eyes need to be trained to scan for hazards in specific areas along your drive path. Looking for hazards along the path of the right side of you vehicle is one of those places.

Look for a bouncing ball that may have a child running after it. Look for a head in the car that may warn of someone opening the door just as you get there to avoid taking the door off with your bumper. Look for other signs of a car about to pull away from the curb or backing out of a driveway by noticing wheels turned out, blinkers on, or exhaust from a tailpipe indicating that the car is started and ready to move.

Try to make eye contact with drivers who are planning to enter the road you are traveling. If you fail to make eye contact, take that as an extra warning that the person has not seen you and may put you in danger.

Look for (and slow down if necessary to get around) bicycle riders who have as much right to be on the road as you are but don't have much protection against injury if involved in a collision.

Many accident statements include, "I just didn't see that car" or "They came out of nowhere" when in truth, they failed to scan properly.

SKILL # 6 HAZARDS ON THE LEFT

Hazards on the Left contain many of the problems Hazards on the Right present and in addition come with special issues. Traffic is coming toward you at a similar speed you are going. You often have only a line down the middle of the road and that offers no protection from a head-on collision - the most deadly kind. In effect, a collision with an oncoming car would be at double the speed and a force that is 4 times greater than if you hit an immovable stationary object on the right. Your decision should always be to avoid the head-on collision.

To avoid a head-on collision in a situation where a collision is inescapable, choose the softest thing on your right to collide with (other than pedestrians) such as bushes or walls choosing them over trees and telephone poles which may not give way, causing you a sudden and terrible stop. Even other cars driving in the lane next to you going about your same speed is a better option than a head-on collision or a sudden stop by a tree.

SKILL # 7 BLIND SPOTS

Always check your blind spot when changing lanes and don't ride in someone's blind spot.

You check your blind spot in the direction you want to go. If you are lane changing to the right, you look quickly over your right shoulder. If you are moving to the left, make a quick look over your left shoulder.

Aside from intersections, the number one cause of accidents on the surface streets and #2 on the freeways is changing lanes. That's because some people don't check their blind spot and others are dumb enough to be in one.

If you can see the driver's face in his side view mirror, the driver can see you. Once the driver's face disappears, you disappear. At that moment, you are in that driver's blind spot. At that point you should slow down, speed up or change lanes. Do not stay in a blind spot. Limit your time there because the driver may only check mirrors when changing lanes and not realize you are there.

When you go to change lanes, always check your blind spot even when you know there is nobody there because someday, there may be.

For Lane Changing: M-S-B-G (pronounced "Ms. Bug")

The process for changing lanes is one of the most important skills you can learn to keep you safe. If you do it consistently until it is a habit, it will protect you against the number one cause of accidents on the surface streets (other than intersections) and number two on the freeways.

Most driver training students in California learned "SMOG" which stands for "Signals, Mirrors, Over-the-Shoulder, Go" and the value of the memory aid, particularly here in Los Angeles "SMOG" made a lot of industry experts choose that over what it really should be.

We didn't compromise. We put it in the right order –MSOG--, the term 'Over-the-shoulder' was replaced by 'blind spot' which is actually more accurate because that is exactly what you're checking. We had students verbalize the steps as they performed them during behind-the-wheel driver training to help our student remember them. The 5 syllable phrase "Over-the-shoulder" takes too long to say AND do because you can't be looking in your blind spot that long. It needs to be a quick look. That is why we used "Mirror, Signals, Blind spot, Go" or "MSBG" for lane changes.

The blind spot is the area that your mirrors don't cover and it is large enough to put a bus in one lane over. So you check your blind spot then you go. Why did we put Mirrors before Signal? Because you really should check your mirrors before you signal to see if there is even a possibility of making the move.

You check your mirrors to see if it is safe and appropriate to signal. You signal in order to 'signal' your intentions to the other drivers letting them know what you plan to do. You do so as a matter of courtesy and safety. Drivers who are allowed to be courteous often are. Give them the opportunity to be courteous by signaling your intention to make a move and they often will be courteous.

Next, you check your blind spot because someday there will be someone dumb enough to ride in your blind spot and you will swear to the officer taking your accident report that that car wasn't there – and yet it was.

The purpose of driving is to get from one place to another is a safe, efficient and economical manner. I know there are competitive drivers out there – those who don't want to signal because they think that [like themselves] if they signal someone will speed up to block them. These drivers are dangerous on the road because they fail to recognize that driving is a cooperative activity; not a competition. They compromise everyone's safety because of this immature and antisocial perception of driving.

There are a few drivers who appear to have developed their driving skills from video games. When drivers can't tell the difference between games and real life they are trouble for everyone on the road.

These drivers are dangerous because, unlike their driving video games,

--weaving in and out of traffic

--tailgating to intimidate the driver ahead to move over

--snaking lights (i.e. Pulling into the right turn lane to speed past drivers when the light changes)

--ignoring good manners and safety practices

--being antisocial on the road

-- driving on sidewalks

doesn't score points in their favor. They can get points alright – points on their driving records and they can spend time in jail or the hospital as well.

There is no such thing as the Chuck E Cheese School of Driving!

With drivers like these taking to the road, it makes learning the skills to avoid The 13 Most Dangerous Traffic Situations even more important to know and use.

SKILL # 8 FRONT SPACE CUSHION

Your following distance should be about 3 seconds behind the car in front of you and 6 seconds in bad weather. Most drivers were taught to use 2 seconds and older drivers were taught to use "One car length for every 10 miles per hour" as their guide. 3 seconds gives you a superior following distance so we encouraged our students to use the 3 second rule.

If someone slides into the space between you and the car in front of you, you are only losing 3 seconds. Remember, driving is supposed to be a cooperative activity. If 50 people change lanes in front of you on a trip, you might lose two and a half minutes. Isn't less than three minutes worth the extra safety you give yourself?

I used to drive an hour and 20 minutes to work when I was teaching driver education so I would count the number of drivers taking advantage of my excellent following distance. The most I ever counted was 17.

I've driven many more miles than most people. As an instructor, I would average about 200 miles a day. Add to that, 114 personal miles a day round-trip to and from home. I've had cars spin out in front of me due to slick roads, a fuel tanker truck explode a few cars ahead of me, a car flip over going down a grade, cars that stopped for no apparent reason and my following distance gave me the time to avoid being involved in a collision.

At 30 miles per hour you should be 144 feet behind the car in front. That's about 3 average house lots and at freeway speeds it should be double that distance although 3 seconds still applies.

The value of the 3 second rule is that it works at any speed. As you speed increases so does the distance you cover per second.

At 30 miles per hour you are traveling at 44 feet per second.

3 seconds X 44 feet per second = 132 feet.

At 60 miles per hour you are traveling at 88 feet per second.

3 X 88 feet per second is 268 feet of following distance.

The beauty of the skill being 3 seconds is you can easily learn to estimate the proper distance by picking a point you think is 3 seconds ahead and then counting one-one-thousand, two-one thousand, three-one thousand and adjust your timing until you learn how far away it is.

If the car in front of you loses power, brakes suddenly, or stops for a six foot invisible rabbit and you hit that car from behind, it's still your fault. Legally, you must be following at a distance that you can safely stop no matter what is happening in front of you.

Remember, you probably won't see many people out there doing it. Most people THINK they are good drivers. We are beginning to know better, right?

SKILL # 9 REAR SPACE CUSHION

The least controllable cushion you have is to the rear. You can still affect the vehicle behind you in subtle ways to limit your risk. If you have a tailgater, it is not wise to brake suddenly. It is acceptable to slow down a little to give you more time to respond to a slow-down in front of you and gradually slow down to give your tailgater enough time to realize that you are slowing and decide to brake without hitting you. By gradually slowing down you save yourself from being hit from behind and the guy behind you will live to tailgate again.

The first choice when being tailgated should be to get out of his way. Tailgaters are dangerous and should be avoided. Don't try to police bad drivers. Teaching bad drivers a lesson is not your job. If you can't get out of the way because of heavy traffic, then you must give yourself room in front of you to compensate for your lack of space to the rear.

Tapping your brake to warn the driver behind you might cause the tailgater to back off a little but you run the risk of angering the tailgater. Angry tailgaters are bad drivers with attitude. Anger, or any strong emotion for that matter, reduces good judgment. Okay, okay, it can make a person downright dumb. Tailgaters are dumb already so angry tailgaters are double-dumb. It is hard to predict what a very dumb driver will do. You can only be sure that it probably won't be smart. Before you brake, check your rear-view mirror so you know how close the vehicle behind you is following. You may have to brake early so you can slow more gradually if a bad driver is behind you.

SKILL # 10 LEFT CUSHION

Having a place to go quickly to the left in the event of someone pulling into your lane is not possible if you don't maintain a space cushion to your left. The reasons someone would pull into your lane while you occupy it are many. The reasons range from inattentive driving caused by texting, drugs, sleep deprivation, or health issues like a sudden stroke or heart attack to deliberate behavior by a person who is distraught, filled by road rage or suicidal.

You won't know when you will need that cushion and there is no way to get that cushion in time when you do need it unless you make a habit of positioning your vehicle so that you have a cushion at all times. To do this, you can speed up or slow down and if that doesn't work, change lanes. The objective is to have an escape route should you suddenly need it.

SKILL # 11 RIGHT CUSHION

A right cushion on the freeway or multilane street is as easy to keep as a cushion on the left. It is harder to keep when you are traveling in the right lane on surface streets because your escape route is often blocked by parked cars and pedestrians. Still, if the path does not contain people you can elect to drive up on the sidewalk rather than be hit from behind or head-on.

SKILL # 12 VIEWING DISTANCE

Part of your visual scan you want to cultivate into a habit is where you look ahead while you're driving. Along with checking your mirror and scanning for Hazards on the Right and left, you need to focus ahead much of the time to assess what traffic is doing and what road condition are on your immediate path. Many new drivers only look ahead to the next car but that isn't enough.

Looking far down the road regularly can warn you of red tail-lights of cars stopping ahead, traffic lanes being eliminated by road design or construction, bicycle riders or other hazards that will require you or traffic ahead of you to make adjustments. Looking far enough in advance gives you time to make your best choices for a safe and smooth action that will get you to your destination without being stressed by an eventful ride. Scan near and far as part of you visual scanning habit.

SKILL # 13 STAY IN THE RIGHT-HAND LANE

If you have a choice, it is best to travel in the middle or right-hand lane because on-coming traffic is such a danger. When you are traveling in the lane closest to the middle, vehicles are passing you going in the opposite direction with only a few feet between you and them. A poorly timed sneeze, a blown tire, a hazard that suddenly appears may send that driver into your lane. Having an extra lane between you and oncoming traffic gives you a little more time to react and the erring driver a chance to recover. I travel in the left lane only when the Hazards on the Right present a greater danger such as bicyclists, cars stopping to parallel park or vehicles turning right. Then I get back over to a safer lane.

AFTER ALL IS SAID AND DONE

Ultimately, only you will decide to make these techniques your habits. If you practice them until they become second nature they will protect you. Often they will protect you without your awareness. Only by the gauge of your driving record can you prove how well you drive. The number of accidents and tickets you receive are your scorecard. Very few accidents are ever completely one driver's fault. Most accidents can be avoided if you drive defensively.

If you make the effort to learn these habits for excellence in driving they will become your shields against poor drivers and unnecessary injuries. These habits will protect the people you love and care about the most. Members of you family, friends and co-workers are your responsibility when you are behind the wheel.

Learning these defensive driving techniques gives you important skills and you will be giving your loved ones and the other drivers on the road with you, uncommon protection when you are driving.

Long after you forget the names of these habits they will be protecting you automatically because they are habits.

I urge you to learn these techniques and review them at least monthly during your first year of driving to see how well you have incorporated them into you driving habits. After that, periodically check your driving against this list and see how close you come to excellence. I try to review at least once a year and occasionally catch my skills slipping so I make the effort to reintroduce the skills back into my normal driving.

Once these driving skills are mastered and you effortlessly do them out of habit, you can truly call yourself an ***extraordinary driver.***

The 13 Most Dangerous Traffic Situations list in shortened form appears on the next page.

1. Make a copy for your reference and keep it in your vehicle.

2. Do NOT read them while driving.

3. Pick one or two to consciously work on each time you drive until you master each of them.

THE 13 MOST DANGEROUS TRAFFIC SITUATIONS
AND HOW TO SURVIVE THEM

Skill # 1 Intersection Control: Cover your brake and look left and right through intersections.

Skill # 2 STP: The Stationary Check: Starting up from a stop, check Signal -Traffic - Pedestrians.

Skill # 3 Stopping Position: Stop where you can see the bottom of both tires or the limit line if you are first in line.

Skill # 4 The Point of No Return: Plan to stop unless you are 100' from the intersection.

Skill # 5 Hazards on the Right: Scan for hazards to your right.

Skill # 6 Hazards on the Left: Scan for hazards to your left.

Skill # 7 Blind Spots: Stay out of them and always check yours when changing lanes or pulling away from a curb.

Skill # 8 Front Space Cushion: Stay at least 3 seconds behind the car in front of you or 6 seconds in bad weather.

Skill # 9 Rear Space Cushion: Check you mirrors and adjust for tailgaters.

Skill # 10 Left Cushion: Speed up, slow down or change lanes.

Skill # 11 Right Cushion: Speed up, slow down or change lanes.

Skill # 12 Viewing Distance: Look far enough in advance to see hazards in the making.

Skill # 13 Stay in the Right-Hand Lanes: Travel as much as possible in the right lanes to avoid head-on collisions.

ABOUT THE AUTHOR

Credentials held during career:

1. *Teen Auto Club Master Instructor*
2. *Licensed Driving Instructor*
3. *Operator License for Auto Club International Driving and Traffic Schools*
4. *Licensed Traffic School Instructor*

Mitch Terrusa left Teen Auto Club when it closed in 1992. Changing careers, he opened the Computer Tutor & Homework Clinic with his wife, Kathy.

His love for both teaching and the computer field, having dabbled with programming since 1978, gave him the impetus to create his own company that incorporates both. He has enjoyed teaching in homes and businesses in the Southern California region ever since.

Often working remotely over the Internet in the past few years, Mitch has gained the freedom to do a little more traveling -- one of the things he and Kathy love most. Currently you can find out what he is up to by visiting his website at ComputerTutor-LA.com.

Mitch and Kathy have raised 11 children between them but that is a story for another day.

For comments or questions please write to:

Mitch Terrusa
P.O. Box 5371
West Hills, CA 91308

39692311R00024

Made in the USA
Middletown, DE
22 January 2017